Love ...

JOHN DONNE

A Phoenix Paperback

The Complete English Poems of John Donne
published in Everyman in 1994

This abridged edition published by Phoenix
a division of Orion Books Ltd
Orion House, 5 Upper St Martin's Lane, London WC2H 9EA

Copyright © J. M. Dent 1996

ISBN 1 85799 571 6

Typeset by CentraCet Ltd, Cambridge
Printed in Great Britain by
Clays Ltd, St Ives plc

Contents

The Flea 1
The good-morrow 2
Song 3
Womans constancy 4
The undertaking 5
The Sunne Rising 6
The Indifferent 7
Loves Usury 8
The Canonization 9
The triple Foole 11
Lovers infinitenesse 12
Song 14
The Legacie 15
A Feaver 16
Aire and Angels 18
Breake of day 19
The Anniversarie 20
A Valediction of my name, in the window 21
Twicknam garden 24

Communitie   25

Loves Growth   26

The Dreame   27

A Valediction of weeping   29

Loves Alchymie   30

The Curse   31

The Message   32

Witchcraft by a picture   33

The Baite   34

The broken heart   35

A Valediction forbidding mourning   37

The Extasie   38

Loves Deitie   41

The Will   42

Loves diet   45

The Primrose   46

The Relique   47

The Dissolution   49

Negative love   50

The Prohibition   50

The Expiration   51

The Paradox   52

A Lecture upon the Shadow   53

Sonnet. The Token   54

[Selfe Love]   55

The Flea

Marke but this flea, and marke in this,
How little that which thou deny'st me is;
It suck'd me first, and now sucks thee,
And in this flea, our two bloods mingled bee;
Thou know'st that this cannot be said
A sinne, nor shame, nor loss of maidenhead,
    Yet this enjoyes before it wooe,
    And pamper'd swells with one blood made of two
    And this, alas, is more then wee would doe.

Oh stay, three lives in one flea spare,
Where wee almost, yea more then maryed are.
This flea is you and I, and this
Our mariage bed, and mariage temple is;
Though parents grudge, and you, w'are met,
And cloystered in these living walls of Jet.
    Though use make you apt to kill mee,
    Let not to that, selfe murder added bee,
    And sacrilege, three sinnes in killing three.

Cruell and sodaine, hast thou since
Purpled thy naile, in blood of innocence?
Wherein could this flea guilty bee,
Except in that drop which it suckt from thee?

Yet thou triumph'st, and saist that thou
Find'st not thy selfe, nor mee the weaker now;
   'Tis true, then learne how false, feares bee;
    Just so much honor, when thou yeeld'st to mee,
    Will wast, as this flea's death tooke life from thee.

The good-morrow

I wonder by my troth, what thou, and I
Did, till we lov'd? were we not wean'd till then?
But suck'd on countrey pleasures, childishly?
Or snorted we in the seaven sleepers den?
T'was so; But this, all pleasures fancies bee
If ever any beauty I did see,
Which I desir'd, and got, t'was but a dreame of thee.

And now good morrow to our waking soules,
Which watch not one another out of feare;
For love, all love of other sights controules,
And makes one little roome, an every where.
Let sea-discoverers to new worlds have gone,
Let Maps to other, worlds on worlds have showne,
Let us possesse one world, each hath one, and is one.

My face in thine eye, thine in mine appeares,
And true plaine hearts doe in the faces rest,
Where can we finde two better hemispheares
Without sharpe North, without declining West?

What ever dyes, was not mixt equally;
If our two loves be one, or, thou and I
Love so alike, that none doe slacken, none can die.

Song

Goe, and catche a falling starre,
    Get with child a mandrake roote,
Tell me, where all past yeares are,
    Or who cleft the Divels foot,
Teach me to heare Mermaides singing,
Or to keep off envies stinging,
                And finde
                What winde
Serves to advance an honest minde.

If thou beest borne to strange sights,
    Things invisible to see,
Ride ten thousand daies and nights,
    Till age snow white haires on thee,
Thou, when thou retorn'st, wilt tell mee
All strange wonders that befell thee,
                And sweare
                No where
Lives a woman true, and faire.

If thou findst one, let mee know,
    Such a Pilgrimage were sweet,

3

Yet doe not, I would not goe,
    Though at next doore wee might meet,
Though shee were true, when you met her,
And last, till you write your letter,
        Yet shee
        Will bee
False, ere I come, to two, or three.

Womans constancy

Now thou hast lov'd me one whole day,
To morrow when thou leav'st, what wilt thou say?
Wilt thou then Antedate some new made vow?
        Or say that now
We are not just those persons, which we were?
Or, that oathes made in reverentiall feare
Of Love, and his wrath, any may forsweare?
Or, as true deaths, true maryages untie,
So lovers contracts, images of those,
Binde but till sleep, deaths image, them unloose?
        Or, your owne end to Justifie,
For having purpos'd change, and falsehood; you
Can have no way but falsehood to be true?
Vaine lunatique, against these scapes I could
        Dispute, and conquer, if I would,
        Which I abstaine to doe,
4   For by to morrow, I may thinke so too.

The undertaking

I have done one braver thing
    Then all the *Worthies* did,
And yet a braver thence doth spring,
    Which is, to keepe that hid.

It were but madnes now t'impart
    The skill of specular stone,
When he which can have learn'd the art,
    To cut it can finde none.

So, if I now should utter this,
    Others (because no more
Such stuffe to worke upon, there is,)
    Would love but as before.

But he who lovelinesse within
    Hath found, all outward loathes,
For he who colour loves, and skinne,
    Loves but their oldest clothes.

If, as I have, you also doe
    Vertue'attir'd in woman see,
And dare love that, and say so too,
    And forget the Hee and Shee;

And if this love, though placed so,
    From prophane men you hide,

Which will no faith on this bestow,
  Or, if they doe, deride:

Then you have done a braver thing
  Then all the *Worthies* did.
And a braver thence will spring
  Which is, to keepe that hid.

The Sunne Rising

Busie old foole, unruly Sunne,
  Why dost thou thus,
Through windowes, and through curtaines call on us?
Must to thy motions lovers seasons run?
  Sawcy pedantique wretch, goe chide
  Late schoole boyes and sowre prentices,
  Goe tell Court-huntsmen, that the King will ride,
  Call countrey ants to harvest offices;
Love, all alike, no season knowes, nor clyme,
Nor houres, dayes, moneths, which are the rags of time.

Thy beames, so reverend, and strong
  Why shouldst thou thinke?
I could eclipse and cloud them with a winke,
But that I would not lose her sight so long:
  If her eyes have not blinded thine,
  Looke, and to morrow late, tell mee,
  Whether both th'India's of spice and Myne

Be where thou leftst them, or lie here with mee.
Aske for those Kings whom thou saw'st yesterday,
And thou shalt heare, All here in one bed lay.

She'is all States, and all Princes, I,
    Nothing else is.
Princes doe but play us, compar'd to this,
All honor's mimique; All wealth alchimie;
    Thou sunne art halfe as happy'as wee,
    In that world's contracted thus.
Thine age askes ease, and since thy duties bee
To warme the world, that's done in warming us.
Shine here to us, and thou art every where;
This bed thy center is, these walls, thy spheare.

The Indifferent

I can love both faire and browne,
Her whom abundance melts, and her whom want betraies,
Her who loves lonenesse best, and her who maskes and
                                                    plaies,
Her whom the country form'd, and whom the town,
Her who beleeves, and her who tries,
Her who still weepes with spungie eyes,
And her who is dry corke, and never cries;
I can love her, and her, and you and you,
I can love any, so she be not true.

Will no other vice content you?
Wil it not serve your turn to do, as did your mothers?
Or have you all old vices spent, and now would finde
                                                out others?
Or doth a feare, that men are true, torment you?
Oh we are not, be not you so,
Let mee, and doe you, twenty know.
Rob mee, but binde me not, and let me goe.
Much I, who came to travaile thorow you,
Grow your fixt subject, because you are true?

Venus heard me sigh this song,
And by Loves sweetest Part, Variety, she swore,
She heard not this till now; and that it should be so no
                                                more.
She went, examin'd, and return'd ere long,
And said, alas, Some two or three
Poore Heretiques in love there bee,
Which thinke to stablish dangerous constancie.
But I have told them, since you will be true,
You shall be true to them, who'are false to you.

Loves Usury

For every houre that thou wilt spare mee now,
        I will allow,
Usurious God of Love, twenty to thee,

When with my browne, my gray haires equall bee;
Till then, Love, let my body raigne, and let
Mee travell, sojourne, snatch, plot, have, forget,
Resume my last yeares relict: thinke that yet
       We'had never met.

Let mee thinke any rivalls letter mine,
       And at next nine
Keepe midnights promise; mistake by the way
The maid, and tell the Lady of that delay;
Onely let mee love none, no, not the sport
From country grasse, to comfitures of Court,
Or cities quelque choses, let report
       My minde transport.

This bargaine's good; if when I'm old, I bee
       Inflam'd by thee,
If thine owne honour, or my shame, or paine,
Thou covet most, at that age thou shalt gaine.
Doe thy will then, then subject and degree,
And fruit of love, Love I submit to thee,
Spare mee till then, I'll beare it, though she bee
       One that loves mee.

The Canonization

For Godsake hold your tongue, and let me love,
  Or chide my palsie, or my gout,

My five gray haires, or ruin'd fortune flout,
   With wealth your state, your minde with Arts
                           improve,
     Take you a course, get you a place,
     Observe his honour, or his grace,
Or the King's reall, or his stamped face
   Contemplate, what you will, approve,
   So you will let me love.

Alas, alas, who's injur'd by my love?
   What merchants ships have my sighs drown'd?
Who saies my teares have overflow'd his ground?
   When did my colds a forward spring remove?
     When did the heats which my veines fill
     Adde one more to the plaguie Bill?
Soldiers finde warres, and Lawyers finde out still
   Litigious men, which quarrels move,
   Though she and I do love.

Call us what you will, wee are made such by love;
   Call her one, mee another flye,
We'are Tapers too, and at our owne cost die,
   And wee in us finde the'Eagle and the dove,
     The Phœnix ridle hath more wit
     By us, we two being one, are it.
So, to one neutrall thing both sexes fit,
   Wee dye and rise the same, and prove
   Mysterious by this love.

Wee can dye by it, if not live by love,
    And if unfit for tombes and hearse
Our legend bee, it will be fit for verse;
    And if no peece of Chronicle wee prove,
        We'll build in sonnets pretty roomes;
        As well a well wrought urne becomes
The greatest ashes, as half-acre tombes,
    And by these hymnes, all shall approve
    Us *Canoniz'd* for Love.

And thus invoke us; You whom reverend love
    Made one anothers hermitage;
You, to whom love was peace, that now is rage,
    Who did the whole worlds soule contract, and drove
        Into the glasses of your eyes
        So made such mirrors, and such spies,
That they did all to you epitomize,
    Countries, Townes, Courts: Beg from above
    A patterne of our love.

The triple Foole

    I am two fooles, I know,
For loving, and for saying so
    In whining Poëtry;
But where's that wiseman, that would not be I,
    If she would not deny?

Then as th'earths inward narrow crooked lanes
Do purge sea waters fretfull salt away,
   I thought, if I could draw my paines,
Through Rimes vexation, I should them allay,
Griefe brought to numbers cannot be so fierce,
For, he tames it, that fetters it in verse.

   But when I have done so,
Some man, his art and voice to show,
   Doth Set and sing my paine,
And, by delighting many, frees againe
   Griefe, which verse did restraine.
To Love, and Griefe tribute of Verse belongs,
But not of such as pleases when'tis read,
   Both are increased by such songs:
For both their triumphs so are published,
And I, which was two fooles, do so grow three;
Who are a little wise, the best fooles bee.

Lovers infinitenesse

If yet I have not all thy love,
Deare, I shall never have it all,
I cannot breath one other sigh, to move;
Nor can intreat one other teare to fall.
And all my treasure, which should purchase thee,

Sighs, teares, and oathes, and letters I have spent,

Yet no more can be due to mee,
Then at the bargaine made was ment,
If then thy gift of love were partiall,
That some to mee, some should to others fall,
   Deare, I shall never have Thee All.

Or if then thou gavest mee all,
All was but All, which thou hadst then,
But if in thy heart, since, there be or shall,
New love created bee, by other men,
Which have their stocks intire, and can in teares,
In sighs, in oathes, and letters outbid mee,
This new love may beget new feares,
For, this love was not vowed by thee,
And yet it was, thy gift being generall,
The ground, thy heart is mine, what ever shall
   Grow there, deare, I should have it all.

Yet I would not have all yet,
Hee that hath all can have no more,
And since my love doth every day admit
New growth, thou shouldst have new rewards in store;
Thou canst not every day give me thy heart,
If thou canst give it, then thou never gavest it:
Loves riddles are, that though thy heart depart,
It stayes at home, and thou with losing savest it:
But wee will have a way more liberall,
Then changing hearts, to joyne them, so wee shall
   Be one, and one anothers All.

Song

Sweetest love, I do not goe,
    For wearinesse of thee,
Nor in hope the world can show
    A fitter Love for mee,
        But since that I
Must dye at last, 'tis best,
To use my selfe in jest
    Thus by fain'd deaths to dye;

Yesternight the Sunne went hence,
    And yet is here to day,
He hath no desire nor sense,
    Nor halfe so short a way:
        Then feare not mee,
But beleeve that I shall make
Speedier journeyes, since I take
    More wings and spurres than hee.

O how feeble is mans power,
    That if good fortune fall,
Cannot adde another houre,
    Nor a lost houre recall!
        But come bad chance,
And wee joyne to'it our strength,
And wee teach it art and length,
    It selfe o'r us to'advance.

When thou sigh'st, thou sigh'st not winde,
    But sigh'st my soule away,
When thou weep'st, unkindly kinde,
    My lifes blood doth decay.
        It cannot bee
That thou lov'st mee, as thou say'st,
If in thine my life thou waste,
    Thou art the best of mee.

Let not thy divining heart
    Forethinke me any ill,
Destiny may take thy part,
    And may thy feares fulfill,
        But thinke that wee
Are but turn'd aside to sleepe;
They who one another keepe
    Alive, ne'r parted bee.

The Legacie

When I dyed last, and, Deare, I dye
    As often as from thee I goe,
    Though it be but an houre agoe,
And Lovers houres be full eternity,
I can remember yet, that I
    Something did say, and something did bestow;

Though I be dead, which sent mee, I should be
Mine owne executor and Legacie.

I heard mee say, Tell her anon,
    That my selfe, (that's you, not I,)
    Did kill me, and when I felt mee dye,
I bid mee send my heart, when I was gone,
But I alas could there finde none,
    When I had ripp'd me, 'and search'd where hearts did
                                                    lye,
It kill'd mee againe, that I who still was true,
In life, in my last Will should cozen you.

Yet I found something like a heart,
    But colours it, and corners had,
    It was not good, it was not bad,
It was intire to none, and few had part.
As good as could be made by art
    It seem'd, and therefore for our losses sad,
I meant to send this heart in stead of mine,
But oh, no man could hold it, for twas thine.

A Feaver

Oh doe not die, for I shall hate
    All women so, when thou art gone,
That thee I shall not celebrate,
    When I remember, thou wast one.

But yet thou canst not die, I know,
    To leave this world behinde, is death,
But when thou from this world wilt goe,
    The whole world vapors with thy breath.

Or if, when thou, the worlds soule, goest,
    It stay, tis but thy carkasse then,
The fairest woman, but thy ghost,
    But corrupt wormes, the worthyest men.

O wrangling schooles, that search what fire
    Shall burne this world, had none the wit
Unto this knowledge to aspire,
    That this her feaver might be it?

And yet she cannot wast by this,
    Nor long beare this torturing wrong,
For much corruption needfull is
    To fuell such a feaver long.

These burning fits but meteors bee,
    Whose matter in thee is soone spent.
Thy beauty, 'and all parts, which are thee,
    Are unchangeable firmament.

Yet 'twas of my minde, seising thee,
    Though it in thee cannot persever.
For I had rather owner bee
    Of thee one houre, than all else ever.

Aire and Angels

Twice or thrice had I loved thee,
Before I knew thy face or name;
So in a voice, so in a shapelesse flame,
Angells affect us oft, and worship'd bee,
    Still when, to where thou wert, I came
Some lovely glorious nothing I did see,
    But since, my soule, whose child love is,
Takes limmes of flesh, and else could nothing doe,
    More subtile than the parent is,
Love must not be, but take a body too,
    And therefore what thou wert, and who
        I did Love aske, and now
That it assume thy body, I allow,
And fixe it selfe in thy lip, eye, and brow.

Whilst thus to ballast love, I thought,
And so more steddily to have gone,
With wares which would sinke admiration,
I saw, I had loves pinnace overfraught,
    Ev'ry thy haire for love to worke upon
Is much too much, some fitter must be sought;
    For, nor in nothing, nor in things
Extreme, and scattring bright, can love inhere;
    Then as an Angell, face, and wings
Of aire, not pure as it, yet pure doth weare,
    So thy love may be my loves spheare;

Just such disparitie
  As it twixt Aire and Angells puritie,
  T'wixt womens love, and mens will ever bee.

Breake of day

'Tis true, 'tis day, what though it be?
O wilt thou therefore rise from me?
Why should we rise, because 'tis light?
Did we lie downe, because t'was night?
Love which in spight of darknesse brought us hether,
Should in despight of light keepe us together.

Light hath no tongue, but is all eye;
If it could speake as well as spie,
This were the worst, that it could say,
That being well, I faine would stay,
And that I lov'd my heart and honor so
That I would not from him, that had them, goe.

Must businesse thee from hence remove?
Oh, that's the worst disease of love,
The poore, the foule, the false, love can
Admit, but not the busied man.
He which hath businesse, and makes love, doth doe
Such wrong, as when a maryed man doth wooe.

All Kings, and all their favorites,
   All glory of honors, beauties, wits,
The Sun it selfe, which makes times, as they passe,
Is elder by a yeare, now, then it was
When thou and I first one another saw:
All other things, to their destruction draw,
   Only our love hath no decay;
This, no to morrow hath, nor yesterday,
Running it never runs from us away,
But truly keepes his first, last, everlasting day.

   Two graves must hide thine and my coarse,
   If one might, death were no divorce,
Alas, as well as other Princes, wee,
(Who Prince enough in one another bee,)
Must leave at last in death, these eyes, and eares,
Oft fed with true oathes, and with sweet salt teares;
   But soules where nothing dwells but love
(All other thoughts being inmates) then shall prove
This, or a love increased there above,
When bodies to their graves, soules from their graves remove.

   And then wee shall be throughly blest,
   But wee no more, then all the rest,
Here upon earth, we'are Kings, and none but wee
Can be such Kings, nor of such subjects bee;
20 Who is so safe as wee? where none can doe

Treason to us, except one of us two.
　True and false feares let us refraine,
Let us love nobly, and live, and adde againe
Yeares and yeares unto yeares, till we attaine
To write threescore, this is the second of our raigne.

A Valediction of my name,
in the window

I

My name engrav'd herein,
Doth contribute my firmnesse to this glasse,
　Which, ever since that charme, hath beene
　As hard, as that which grav'd it, was,
Thine eye will give it price enough, to mock
　The diamonds of either rock.

II

'Tis much that glasse should bee
As all confessing, and through-shine as I,
　'Tis more, that it shewes thee to thee,
　And cleare refects thee to thine eye.
But all such rules, loves magique can undoe,
　Here you see me, and I am you.

III

As no one point, nor dash,
Which are but accessaries to this name,

The showers and tempests can outwash,
   So shall all times finde mee the same;
You this intirenesse better may fulfill,
     Who have the patterne with you still.

IV

   Or if too hard and deepe
This learning be, for a scratch'd name to teach,
   It, as a given deaths head keepe,
   Lovers mortalitie to preach,
Or thinke this ragged bony name to bee
     My ruinous Anatomie.

V

   Then, as all my soules bee,
Emparadis'd in you, (in whom alone
   I understand, and grow and see,)
   The rafters of my body, bone
Being still with you, the Muscle, Sinew, and Veine,
     Which tile this house, will come againe.

VI

   Till my returne, repaire
And recompact my scattered body so.
   As all the vertuous powers which are
   Fix'd in the starres, are said to flow,
Into such characters, as graved bee
     When these starres have supremacie:

VII

So since this name was cut
When love and griefe their exaltation had,
   No doore 'gainst this names influence shut,
    As much more loving, as more sad,
'Twill make thee; and thou shouldst, till I returne,
      Since I die daily, daily mourne.

VIII

When thy inconsiderate hand
Flings ope this casement, with my trembling name,
   To looke on one, whose wit or land,
    New battry to thy heart may frame,
Then thinke this name alive, and that thou thus
      In it offendst my Genius.

IX

And when thy melted maid,
Corrupted by thy Lover's gold, and page,
   His letter at thy pillow'hath laid,
    Disputed it, and tam'd thy rage,
And thou begin'st to thaw towards him, for this,
      May my name step in, and hide his.

X

And if this treason goe
To an overt act, and that thou write againe;
   In superscribing, this name flow
    Into thy fancy, from the pane.

So, in forgetting thou remembrest right,
	And unaware to mee shalt write.

XI

But glasse, and lines must bee,
No meanes our firme substantiall love to keepe;
	Neere death inflicts this lethargie,
	And this I murmure in my sleepe;
Impute this idle talke, to that I goe,
	For dying men talke often so.

Twicknam garden

Blasted with sighs, and surrounded with teares,
	Hither I come to seeke the spring,
	And at mine eyes, and at mine eares,
Receive such balmes, as else cure every thing,
	But O, selfe traytor, I do bring
The spider love, which transubstantiates all,
	And can convert Manna to gall,
And that this place may thoroughly be thought
	True Paradise, I have the serpent brought.

'Twere wholsomer for mee, that winter did
	Benight the glory of this place,
	And that a grave frost did forbid
These trees to laugh and mocke mee to my face;
	But that I may not this disgrace

Indure, nor yet leave loving, Love let mee
   Some senslesse peece of this place bee;
Make me a mandrake, so I may grow here,
   Or a stone fountaine weeping out my yeare.

Hither with christall vyals, lovers come,
   And take my teares, which are loves wine,
   And try your mistresse Teares at home,
For all are false, that tast not just like mine;
   Alas, hearts do not in eyes shine,
Nor can you more judge womans thoughts by teares,
   Then by her shadow, what she weares.
O perverse sexe, where none is true but shee,
   Who's therefore true, because her truth kills mee.

Communitie

Good wee must love, and must hate ill,
   For ill is ill, and good good still,
     But there are things indifferent,
Which wee may neither hate, nor love,
But one, and then another prove,
     As wee shall finde our fancy bent.

If then at first wise Nature had
Made women either good or bad,
     Then some wee might hate, and some chuse,
But since shee did them so create,

That we may neither love, nor hate,
  Onely this rests, All, all may use.

If they were good it would be seene,
Good is as visible as greene,
  And to all eyes it selfe betrayes,
If they were bad, they could not last,
Bad doth it selfe, and others wast,
  So, they deserve nor blame, nor praise.

But they are ours as fruits are ours,
He that but tasts, he that devours,
  And he that leaves all, doth as well,
Chang'd loves are but chang'd sorts of meat,
And when he hath the kernell eate,
  Who doth not fling away the shell?

Loves growth

I scarce beleeve my love to be so pure
    As I had thought it was,
    Because it doth endure
Vicissitude, and season, as the grasse;
Me thinkes I lyed all winter, when I swore,
My love was infinite, if spring make'it more.
But if this medicine, love, which cures all sorrow
With more, not onely bee no quintessence,
But mixt of all stuffes, paining soule, or sense,

26

And of the Sunne his working vigour borrow,
Love's not so pure, and abstract, as they use
To say, which have no Mistresse but their Muse,
But as all else, being elemented too,
Love sometimes would contemplate, sometimes do.

And yet no greater, but more eminent
    Love by the Spring is growne;
    As, in the firmament,
Starres by the Sunne are not inlarg'd, but showne,
Gentle love deeds, as blossomes on a bough,
From loves awakened root do bud out now.
If, as in water stir'd more circles bee
Produc'd by one, love such additions take,
Those like so many spheares, but one heaven make,
For, they are all concentrique unto thee,
And though each spring doe adde to love new heate,
As princes doe in times of action get
New taxes, and remit them not in peace,
No winter shall abate the springs encrease.

The Dreame

Deare love, for nothing lesse then thee
Would I have broke this happy dreame,
      It was a theame
For reason, much too strong for phantasie,

Therefore thou wakd'st me wisely; yet
My Dreame thou brok'st not, but continued'st it,
Thou art so truth, that thoughts of thee suffice,
To make dreames truths; and fables histories;
Enter these armes, for since thou thoughtst it best,
Not to dreame all my dreame, let's act the rest.

As lightning, or a Tapers light,
Thine eyes, and not thy noise wak'd mee;
       Yet I thought thee
(For thou lovest truth) an Angell, at first sight,
But when I saw thou sawest my heart,
And knew'st my thoughts, beyond an Angels art,
When thou knew'st what I dreamt, when thou knew'st
                       when
Excess of joy would wake me, and cam'st then,
I must confesse, it could not chuse but bee
Prophane, to thinke thee any thing but thee.

Comming and staying show'd thee, thee,
But rising makes me doubt, that now,
       Thou art not thou.
That love is weake, where feare's as strong as hee;
'Tis not all spirit, pure, and brave,
If mixture it of *Feare, Shame, Honor*, have;
Perchance as torches which must ready bee,
Men light and put out, so thou deal'st with mee,
Thou cam'st to kindle, goest to come; Then I
28 Will dreame that hope againe, but else would die.

A Valediction of weeping

       Let me powre forth
My teares before thy face, whil'st I stay here,
For thy face coines them, and thy stampe they beare,
And by this Mintage they are something worth,
       For thus they bee
       Pregnant of thee,
Fruits of much griefe they are, emblemes of more,
When a teare falls, that thou falst which it bore,
So thou and I are nothing then, when on a divers shore.

       On a round ball
A workeman that hath copies by, can lay
An Europe, Afrique, and an Asia,
And quickly make that, which was nothing, *All*,
       So doth each teare,
       Which thee doth weare,
A globe, yea world by that impression grow,
Till thy teares mixt with mine doe overflow
This world, by waters sent from thee, my heaven
dissolved so.

       O more then Moone,
Draw not up seas to drowne me in thy spheare,
Weepe me not dead, in thine armes, but forbeare
To teach the sea, what it may doe too soone,
       Let not the winde
       Example finde,

To doe me more harme, then it purposeth,
Since thou and I sigh one anothers breath,
Who e'r sighes most, is cruellest, and hastes the others
                                                        death.

Loves Alchymie

Some that have deeper digg'd loves Myne then I,
Say, where his centrique happinesse doth lie:
     I have lov'd, and got, and told,
But should I love, get, tell, till I were old,
I should not finde that hidden mysterie;
     Oh, 'tis imposture all:
And as no chymique yet th'Elixar got,
     But glorifies his pregnant pot,
     If by the way to him befall
Some odoriferous thing, or medicinall,
  So, lovers dreame a rich and long delight,
   But get a winter-seeming summers night.

Our ease, our thrift, our honor, and our day,
Shall we, for this vaine Bubles shadow pay?
     Ends love in this, that my man,
Can be as happy'as I can; If he can
Endure the short scorne of a Bridgegroomes play?
     That loving wretch that sweares,
30 'Tis not the bodies marry, but the mindes,

Which he in her Angelique findes,
       Would sweare as justly, that he heares,
In that dayes rude hoarse minstralsey, the spheares.
   Hope not for minde in women; at their best,
   Sweetnesse, and wit they'are, but, *Mummy*, possest.

The Curse

Who ever guesses, thinks, or dreames he knowes
Who is my mistris, wither by this curse;
       His only, and only his purse
       May some dull heart to love dispose,
And shee yeeld then to all that are his foes;
   May he be scorn'd by one, whom all else scorne,
   Forsweare to others, what to her he'hath sworne,
   With feare of missing, shame of getting torne;

Madnesse his sorrow, gout his cramp, may hee
Make, by but thinking, who hath made him such:
       And may he feele no touch
       Of conscience, but of fame, and bee
Anguish'd, not that'swas sinne, but that'swas shee:
   In early and long scarceness may he rot,
   For land which had been his, if he had not
   Himselfe incestuously an heire begot:

May he dreame Treason, and beleeve, that hee
Meant to performe it, and confesse, and die,

And no record tell why:
His sonnes, which none of his may bee,
Inherite nothing but his infamie:
Or may he so long Parasites have fed,
That he would faine be theirs, whom he hath bred,
And at the last be circumcis'd for bread:

The venom of all stepdames, gamsters gall,
What Tyrans, and their subjects interwish,
What Plants, Myne, Beasts, Foule, Fish,
Can contribute, all ill, which all
Prophets, or Poets spake; And all which shall
Be annex'd in schedules unto this by mee,
Fall on that man; For if it be a shee
Nature beforehand hath out-cursed mee.

The Message

Send home my long strayd eyes to mee,
Which (Oh) too long have dwelt on thee,
Yet since there they have learn'd such ill,
Such forc'd fashions,
And false passions.
That they be
Made by thee
Fit for no good sight, keep them still.

Send home my harmlesse heart againe,
Which no unworthy thought could staine,
Which if it be taught by thine
  To make jestings
  Of protestings,
   And breake both
   Word and oath,
Keepe it, for then 'tis none of mine.

Yet send me back my heart and eyes,
That I may know, and see thy lyes,
And may laugh and joy, when thou
  Art in anguish
  And dost languish
   For some one
   That will none,
Or prove as false as thou art now.

Witchcraft by a picture

I fixe mine eye on thine, and there
 Pitty my picture burning in thine eye,
My picture drown'd in a transparent teare,
 When I looke lower I espie,
  Hadst thou the wicked skill
By pictures made and mard, to kill,
How many wayes mightst thou performe thy will? 33

But now I have drunke thy sweet salt teares,
  And though thou poure more I'll depart;
My picture vanish'd, vanish feares,
  That I can be endamag'd by that art;
    Though thou retaine of mee
One picture more, yet that will bee,
Being in thine owne heart, from all malice free.

The Baite

Come live with mee, and bee my love,
And wee will some new pleasures prove
Of golden sands, and christall brookes:
With silken lines, and silver hookes.

There will the river whispering runne
Warm'd by thy eyes, more than the Sunne.
And there the'inamor'd fish will stay,
Begging themselves they may betray.

When thou wilt swimme in that live bath,
Each fish, which every channell hath,
Will amorously to thee swimme,
Gladder to catch thee, than thou him.

If thou, to be so seene, beest loath,
By Sunne, or Moone, thou darknest both,

And if my-selfe have leave to see,
I need not their light, having thee.

Let others freeze with angling reeds,
And cut their legges, with shells and weeds,
Or treacherously poore fish beset,
With strangling snare, or windowie net:

Let coarse bold hands, from slimy nest
The bedded fish in banks out-wrest,
Or curious traitors, sleavesilke flies
Bewitch poore fishes wandring eyes.

For thee, thou needst no such deceit,
For thou thy selfe art thine owne bait,
That fish, that is not catch'd thereby,
Alas, is wiser farre than I.

The broken heart

He is starke mad, who ever sayes,
    That he hath been in love an houre,
Yet not that love so soone decayes,
    But that it can tenne in lesse space devour;
Who will beleeve mee, if I sweare
That I have had the plague a yeare?
    Who would not laugh at mee, if I should say,
    I saw a flaske of *powder burne a day*?

Ah, what a trifle is a heart,
  If once into lovers hands it come!
All other griefes allow a part
  To other griefes, and aske themselves but some,
They come to us, but us Love draws,
Hee swallows us, and never chawes:
    By him, as by chain'd shot, whole rankes doe dye,
    He is the tyran Pike, our hearts the Frye.

If 'twere not so, what did become
  Of my heart, when I first saw thee?
I brought a heart into the roome,
  But from the roome, I carried none with mee;
If it had gone to thee, I know
Mine would have taught thine heart to show
    More pitty unto mee: but Love, alas
    At one first blow did shiver it as glasse.

Yet nothing can to nothing fall,
  Nor any place be empty quite,
Therefore I thinke my breast hath all
  Those peeces still, though they be not unite;
And now as broken glasses show
A hundred lesser faces, so
    My ragges of heart can like, wish, and adore,
    But after one such love, can love no more.

A Valediction forbidding mourning

As virtuous men passe mildly away,
  And whisper to their soules, to goe,
Whilst some of their sad friends doe say,
  The breath goes now, and some say, no.

So let us melt, and make no noise,
  No teare-floods, nor sigh-tempests move,
T'were prophanation of our joyes,
  To tell the layetie our love.

Moving of th'earth brings harmes and feares,
  Men reckon what it did and meant,
But trepidation of the spheares,
  Though greater farre, is innocent.

Dull sublunary lovers love
  (Whose soule is sense) cannot admit
Absence, because it doth remove
  Those things which elemented it.

But we by a love, so much refin'd,
  That our selves know not what it is,
Inter-assured of the mind,
  Care lesse, eyes, lips, hands to misse.

Our two soules therefore, which are one,
  Though I must goe, endure not yet

A breach, but an expansion,
    Like gold to ayery thinnesse beate.

If they be two, they are two so
    As stiffe twin compasses are two,
Thy soule the fixt foot, makes no show
    To move, but doth, if the'other doe.

And though it in the center sit,
    Yet when the other far doth rome,
It leanes, and hearkens after it,
    And growes erect, as that comes home.

Such wilt thou be to mee, who must
    Like th'other foot, obliquely runne.
Thy firmnes makes my circle just,
    And makes me end, where I begunne.

The Extasie

Where, like a pillow on a bed,
    A Pregnant banke swel'd up, to rest
The violets reclining head,
    Sat we two, one anothers best;
Our hands were firmely cimented
    With a fast balme, which thence did spring,
Our eye-beames twisted, and did thred
Our eyes, upon one double string,

So to'entergraft our hands, as yet
    Was all the meanes to make us one,
And pictures in our eyes to get
    Was all our propagation.
As 'twixt two equall Armies, Fate
    Suspends uncertaine victorie,
Our soules, (which to advance their state,
    Were gone out,) hung 'twixt her, and mee.
And whil'st our soules negotiate there,
    Wee like sepulchrall statues lay,
All day, the same our postures were,
    And wee said nothing, all the day.
If any, so by love refin'd,
    That he soules language understood,
And by good love were growen all minde,
    Within convenient distance stood,
He (though he knowes not which soul spake,
    Because both meant, both spake the same)
Might thence a new concoction take,
    And part farre purer then he came.
This Extasie doth unperplex
    (We said) and tell us what we love,
Wee see by this, it was not sexe
    Wee see, we saw not what did move:
But as all severall soules containe
    Mixture of things, they know not what,
Love, these mixt soules, doth mixe againe,
    And makes both one, each this and that.

A single violet transplant,
   The strength, the colour, and the size,
(All which before was poore, and scant,)
   Redoubles still, and multiplies.
When love, with one another so
   Interinanimates two soules,
That abler soule, which thence doth flow,
   Defects of loneliness controules.
Wee then, who are this new soule, know,
   Of what we are compos'd, and made,
For, th'Atomies of which we grow,
   Are soules, whom no change can invade.
But O alas, so long, so farre
   Our bodies why doe wee forbeare?
They are ours, though not wee, Wee are
   The intelligences, they the spheares.
We owe them thankes, because they thus,
   Did us, to us, at first convay,
Yeelded their senses force to us,
   Nor are drosse to us, but allay.
On man heavens influence workes not so,
   But that it first imprints the ayre,
For soule into the soule may flow,
   Though it to body first repaire.
As our blood labours to beget
   Spirits, as like soules as it can,
Because such fingers need to knit
   That subtile knot, which makes us man:

So much pure lovers soules descend
    T'affections, and to faculties,
Which sense may reach and apprehend,
    Else a great Prince in prison lies.
To'our bodies turne wee then, that so
    Weake men on love reveal'd may looke;
Loves mysteries in soules doe grow,
    But yet the body is his booke.
And if some lover, such as wee,
    Have heard this dialogue of one,
Let him still marke us, he shall see
    Small change, when we'are to bodies gone.

Loves Deitie

I long to talke with some old lovers ghost,
    Who dyed before the god of Love was borne:
I cannot thinke that hee, who then lov'd most,
    Sunke so low, as to love one which did scorne.
But since this god produc'd a destinie,
And that vice-nature, custome, lets it be;
    I must love her, that loves not mee.

Sure, they which made him god, meant not so much:
    Nor he, in his young godhead practis'd it.
But when an even flame two hearts did touch,
    His office was indulgently to fit

Actives to passives. Correspondencie
Only his subject was; It cannot bee
  Love, till I love her, that loves mee.

But every moderne god will now extend
  His vast prerogative, as far as Jove.
To rage, to lust, to write to, to commend,
  All is the purlewe of the God of Love.
Oh were wee wak'ned by this Tyrannie
To ungod this child againe, it could not bee
  I should love her, who loves not mee.

Rebell and Atheist too, why murmure I,
  As though I felt the worst that love could doe?
Love may make me leave loving, or might trie
  A deeper plague, to make her love mee too,
Which since she loves before, I'am loth to see;
Falsehood is worse than hate; and that must bee
  If shee whom I love, should love mee.

The Will

Before I sigh my last gaspe, let me breath,
Great love, some Legacies: Here I bequeath
Mine eyes to *Argus*, if mine eyes can see,
If they be blinde, then Love, I give them thee;
My tongue to Fame; to'Embassadours mine eares;
  To women or the sea, my tears;

Thou, Love, hast taught mee heretofore
By making mee serve her who'had twenty more,
That I should give to none, but such, as had too much
before.

My constancie I to the planets give,
My truth to them, who at the Court doe live;
Mine ingenuity and opennesse,
To Jesuites; to Buffones my pensivenesse;
My silence to'any, who abroad hath beene;
My mony to a Capuchin.
Thou Love taught'st me, by appointing mee
To love there, where no love receiv'd can be,
Onely to give to such as have an incapacitie.

My faith I give to Roman Catholiques;
All my goods works unto the Schismaticks
Of Amsterdam: my best civility
And Courtship, to an Universitie;
My modesty I give to souldiers bare;
My patience let gamesters share.
Thou Love taughtst mee, by making mee
Love her that holds my love disparity,
Onely to give to those that count my gifts indignity.

I give my reputation to those
Which were my friends; Mine industrie to foes;
To Schoolemen I bequeath my doubtfulnesse;
My sicknesse to Physitians, or excesse;

To Nature, all that I in Ryme have writ;
   And to my company my wit;
Thou love, by making mee adore
Her, who begot this love in mee before,
Taughtst me to make, as though I gave, when I did but
                                             restore.

To him for whom the passing bell next tolls,
   I give my physick bookes; my writen rowles
Of Morall counsels, I to Bedlam give;
My brazen medals, unto them which live
In want of bread; To them which passe among
   All forrainers, mine English tongue.
Thou, Love, by making mee love one
Who thinkes her friendship a fit portion
For yonger lovers, dost my gifts thus disproportion.

Therefore I'll give no more; But I'll undoe
My world by dying; because love dies too.
Then all your beauties wil be no more worth
Then gold in Mines, where none doth draw it forth.
And all your graces no more use shall have
   Then a Sun dyall in a grave,
Thou Love taughtst mee, by making mee
Love her, who doth neglect both mee and thee,
To'invent, and practise this one way, to'annihilate all
                                             three.

Loves diet

To what a combersome unwieldinesse
And burdenous corpulence my love had growne,
   But that I did, to make it lesse,
   And keepe it in proportion,
Give it a diet, made it feed upon
That which love worst endures, *discretion*.

Above one sigh a day I'allow'd him not,
Of which my fortune, and my faults had part;
   And if sometimes by stealth he got
   A she sigh from my mistresse heart,
And thought to feast on that, I let him see
'Twas neither very sound, nor meant to mee;

If he wroung from mee'a teare, I brin'd it so
With scorne or shame, that him it nourish'd not;
   If he suck'd hers, I let him know,
   'Twas not a teare, which hee had got,
His drinke was counterfeit, as was his meat;
For, eyes which rowle towards all, weepe not, but sweat.

What ever he would dictate, I writ that,
But burnt my letters; When she writ to me,
   And that that favour made him fat,
   I said, if any title bee
Convey'd by this, Ah, what doth it availe,
To be the fortieth name in an entaile?

Thus I reclaim'd my buzard love, to flye
At what, and when, and how, and where I chuse;
   Now negligent of sports I lye,
   And now as other Fawkners use,
I spring a mistresse, sweare, write, sigh and weepe:
And the game kill'd, or lost, goe talke, and sleepe.

The Primrose

     Upon this Primrose Hill
     Where, if Heav'n would distill
A shoure of raine, each severall drop might goe
To his owne primrose, and grow Manna so;
And where their forme, and their infinitie
     Make a terrestriall Galaxie,
     As the small starres doe in the skie:
I walke to finde a true Love; and I see
That'tis not a mere woman, that is shee,
But must, or more, or lesse then woman bee.

     Yet know I not, which flower
     I wish; a sixe, or foure;
For should my true-Love lesse than woman bee,
She were scarce any thing; and then, should she
Be more then woman, shee would get above
     All thought of sexe, and thinke to move
     My heart to study her, and not to love;

Both these were monsters; Since there must reside
Falsehood in woman, I could more abide,
She were by art, then Nature falsify'd.

      Live Primrose then, and thrive
        With thy true number five;
And women, whom this flower doth represent,
With this mysterious number be content;
Ten is the farthest number, if halfe ten
        Belongs unto each woman, then
        Each woman may take halfe us men,
Or if this will not serve their turne, Since all
Numbers are odde, or even, and they fall
First into this five, women may take us all.

The Relique

      When my grave is broke up againe
      Some second ghest to entertaine,
      (For graves have learn'd that woman-head
      To be to more then one a Bed)
        And he that digs it, spies
A bracelet of bright haire about the bone,
        Will he not let'us alone,
And thinke that there a loving couple lies,
Who thought that this device might be some way

To make their soules, at the last busie day,
Meet at this grave, and make a little stay?

>   If this fall in a time, or land,
>   When mis-devotion doth command,
>   Then, he that digges us up, will bring
>   Us, to the Bishop, and the King,
>   To make us Reliques; then
> Thou shalt be a Mary Magdalen, and I
>   A something else thereby;
> All women shall adore us, and some men;
> And since at such time, miracles are sought,
> I would have that age by this paper taught
> What miracles wee harmlesse lovers wrought.

>   First, we lov'd well and faithfully,
>   Yet knew not what wee lov'd, nor why,
>   Difference of sex no more wee knew,
>   Then our Guardian Angells doe,
>   Comming and going, wee,
> Perchance might kisse, but not between those meales.
>   Our hands ne'r toucht the seales,
> Which nature, injur'd by late law, sets free,
> These miracles wee did; but now alas,
> All measure, and all language, I should passe,
> Should I tell what a miracle shee was.

The Dissolution

Shee'is dead; And all which die
   To their first Elements resolve;
And wee were mutuall Elements to us,
      And made of one another.
  My body then doth hers involve,
And those things whereof I consist, hereby
In me abundant grow, and burdenous,
      And nourish not, but smother.
  My fire of Passion, sighes of ayre,
Water of teares, and earthly sad despaire,
      Which my materialls bee,
But ne'r worne out by loves securitie,
Shee, to my losse, doth by her death repaire,
   And I might live long wretched so
But that my fire doth with my fuell grow.
      Now as those Active Kings
   Whose foraine conquest treasure brings,
Receive more, and spend more, and soonest breake:
This (which I am amaz'd that I can speake)
     This death, hath with my store
      My use encreas'd.
And so my soule more earnestly releas'd,
Will outstrip hers; As bullets flowen before
A latter bullet may o'rtake, the pouder being more.

Negative love

I never stoop'd so low, as they
Which on an eye, cheeke, lip, can prey,
   Seldome to them, which soare no higher
   Then vertue or the minde to'admire,
For sense, and understanding may
   Know, what gives fuell to their fire:
My love, though silly, is more brave,
For may I misse, when ere I crave,
If I know yet, what I would have.

If that be simply perfectest
Which can by no way be exprest
   But *Negatives*, my love is so.
   To All, which all love, I say no.
If any who deciphers best,
   What we know not, our selves, can know,
Let him teach mee that nothing; This
As yet my ease, and comfort is,
Though I speed not, I cannot misse.

The Prohibition

Take heed of loving mee,
At least remember, I forbade it thee;
Not that I shall repaire my'unthrifty wast

Of Breath and Blood, upon thy sighes, and teares,
By being to mee then that which thou wast,
But, so great Joy, our life at once outweares,
Then, least thy love, by my death, frustrate bee,
If thou love mee, take heed of loving mee.

      Take heed of hating mee,
Or too much triumph in the Victorie.
Not that I shall be mine owne officer,
And hate with hate againe retaliate;
But thou wilt lose the stile of conquerour,
If I, thy conquest, perish by thy hate.
Then, least my being nothing lessen thee,
If thou hate mee, take heed of hating mee.

      Yet, love and hate mee too,
So, these extreames shall ne'r their office doe;
Love mee, that I may die the gentler way;
Hate mee, because thy love is too great for mee;
Or let these two, themselves, not me decay;
So shall I live thy stay, not triumph bee;
Lest thou thy love and hate and mee undoe,
To let mee live, Oh love and hate mee too.

The Expiration

So, so, breake off this last lamenting kisse,
  Which sucks two soules, and vapors Both away,

Turne thou ghost that way, and let mee turne this,
  And let our selves benight our happiest day,
We aske none leave to love; nor will we owe
  Any, so cheape a death, as saying, Goe;

Goe; and if that word have not quite kil'd thee,
  Ease mee with death, by bidding mee goe too.
Oh, if it have, let my word worke on mee,
  And a just office on a murderer doe.
Except it be too late, to kill me so,
  Being double dead, going, and bidding, goe.

The Paradox

No Lover saith, I love, nor any other
    Can judge a perfect Lover;
Hee thinks that else none can or will agree,
    That any loves but hee:
I cannot say I lov'd, for who can say
    Hee was kill'd yesterday.
Love with excesse of heat, more yong then old,
    Death kills with too much cold;
Wee dye but once, and who lov'd last did die,
    Hee that saith twice, doth lye:
For though hee seeme to move, and stirre a while,
    It doth the sense beguile.
Such life is like the light which bideth yet

When the lifes light is set,
Or like the heat, which fire in solid matter
    Leaves behinde, two houres after.
Once I lov'd and dyed; and am now become
    Mine Epitaph and Tombe.
Here dead men speake their last, and so do I;
    Love-slaine, loe, here I dye.

A Lecture upon the Shadow

Stand still, and I will read to thee
A Lecture, Love, in loves philosophy.
    These three houres that we have spent,
    Walking here, Two shadowes went
Along with us, which we our selves produc'd;
But, now the Sunne is just above our head,
    We doe those shadowes tread;
    And to brave clearnesse all things are reduc'd.
  So whilst our infant loves did grow,
  Disguises did, and shadowes, flow,
  From us, and our cares; but, now 'tis not so.

That love hath not attain'd the high'st degree,
Which is still diligent lest others see.

Except our loves at this noone stay,
We shall new shadowes make the other way.
    As the first were made to blinde

Others; these which come behinde
Will worke upon our selves, and blind our eyes.
If our loves faint, and westwardly decline;.
    To me thou, falsly, thine,
        And I to thee mine actions shall disguise.
    The morning shadowes weare away,
    But these grow longer all the day,
    But oh, loves day is short, if love decay.

Love is a growing, or full constant light;
And his first minute, after noone, is night.

Sonnet. The Token

Send me some tokens, that my hope may live,
    Or that my easelesse thoughts may sleep and rest;
Send me some honey to make sweet my hive,
    That in my passions I may hope the best.
I beg noe ribbond wrought with thine owne hands,
    To knit our loves in the fantastick straine
Of new-toucht youth; nor Ring to shew the stands
    Of our affection, that as that's round and plaine,
So should our loves meet in simplicity.
    No, nor the Coralls which thy wrist infold,
Lac'd up together in congruity,
    To shew our thoughts should rest in the same hold,
No, nor thy picture, though most gracious,

And most desir'd 'cause 'tis like thee best;
Nor witty Lines, which are most copious,
   Within the Writings which thou has addrest.

Send me nor this, nor that, t'increase my score,
But swear thou thinkst I love thee, and no more.

[*Selfe Love*]

He that cannot chuse but love,
  And strives against it still,
Never shall my fancy move;
  For he loves agaynst his will;
Nor he which is all his own,
  And can att pleasure chuse,
When I am caught he can be gone,
  And when he list refuse.
Nor he that loves none but faire,
  For such by all are sought;
Nor he that can for foul ones care,
  For his Judgement then is nought:
Nor he that hath wit, for he
  Will make me his jest or slave
Nor a fool for when others, . . .
  He can neither . . .
Nor he that still his Mistresse payes,
  For she is thrall'd therefore:

Nor he that payes not, for he sayes
Within shee's worth no more.
Is there then no kinde of men
Whom I may freely prove?
I will vent that humour then
In mine own selfe love.

PHOENIX 60P PAPERBACKS

HISTORY/BIOGRAPY/TRAVEL
The Empire of Rome A.D. 98–190 *Edward Gibbon*
The Prince *Machiavelli*
The Alan Clark Diaries: Thatcher's Fall *Alan Clark*
Churchill: Embattled Hero *Andrew Roberts*
The French Revolution *E.J. Hobsbawm*
Voyage Around the Horn *Joshua Slocum*
The Great Fire of London *Samuel Pepys*
Utopia *Thomas More*
The Holocaust *Paul Johnson*
Tolstoy and History *Isaiah Berlin*

SCIENCE AND PHILOSOPHY
A Guide to Happiness *Epicurus*
Natural Selection *Charles Darwin*
Science, Mind & Cosmos *John Brockman, ed.*
Zarathustra *Friedrich Nietzsche*
God's Utility Function *Richard Dawkins*
Human Origins *Richard Leakey*
Sophie's World: The Greek Philosophers *Jostein Gaarder*
The Rights of Woman *Mary Wollstonecraft*
The Communist Manifesto *Karl Marx & Friedrich Engels*
Birds of Heaven *Ben Okri*

FICTION
Riot at Misri Mandi *Vikram Seth*
The Time Machine *H. G. Wells*

Love in the Night *F. Scott Fitzgerald*
The Murders in the Rue Morgue *Edgar Allan Poe*
The Necklace *Guy de Maupassant*
You Touched Me *D. H. Lawrence*
The Mabinogion *Anon*
Mowgli's Brothers *Rudyard Kipling*
Shancarrig *Maeve Binchy*
A Voyage to Lilliput *Jonathan Swift*

POETRY
Songs of Innocence and Experience *William Blake*
The Eve of Saint Agnes *John Keats*
High Waving Heather *The Brontes*
Sailing to Byzantium *W. B. Yeats*
I Sing the Body Electric *Walt Whitman*
The Ancient Mariner *Samuel Taylor Coleridge*
Intimations of Immortality *William Wordsworth*
Palgrave's Golden Treasury of Love Poems *Francis Palgrave*
Goblin Market *Christina Rossetti*
Fern Hill *Dylan Thomas*

LITERATURE OF PASSION
Don Juan *Lord Byron*
From Bed to Bed *Catullus*
Satyricon *Petronius*
Love Poems *John Donne*
Portrait of a Marriage *Nigel Nicolson*
The Ballad of Reading Gaol *Oscar Wilde*
Love Sonnets *William Shakespeare*
Fanny Hill *John Cleland*
The Sexual Labyrinth (for women) *Alina Reyes*
Close Encounters (for men) *Alina Reyes*